Brown Bear or Black Bear?

Heather Warren & Robbie Byerly

This is a brown bear.

This is a black bear.

But some black bears are brown.

And some brown bears are black.

How can you see if it is a brown
bear or a black bear?

Here is how.

4 feet

A brown bear is big.

2 ¹/₂ feet

A black bear is not as big.

back

A brown bear looks like this.

back

A black bear looks like this.

ear

A brown bear has little ears.
The ears look like this.

ear

A black bear has big ears.
The ears look like this.

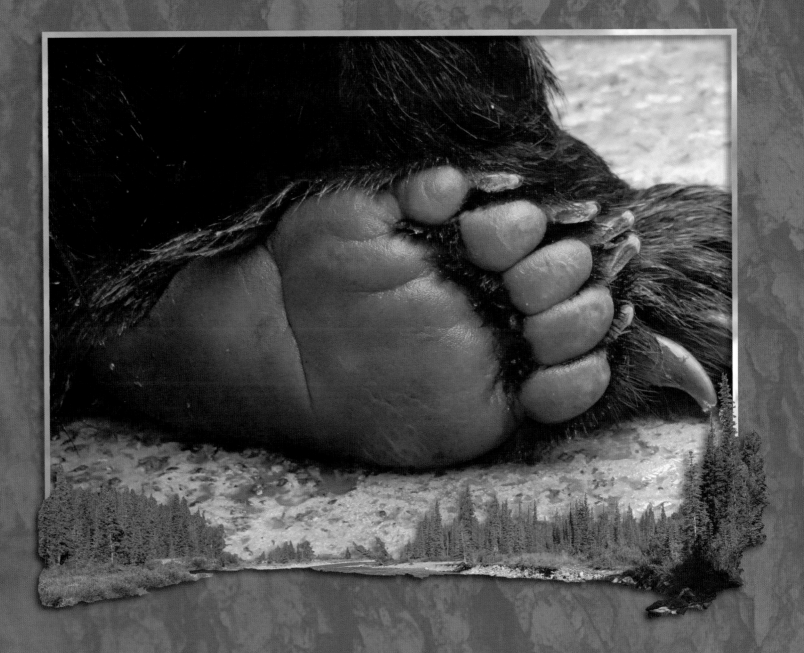

Brown bears have big paws.

Black bears have little paws.

Brown bears like to eat lots of fish.

Black bears like to eat berries and honey. 17

Brown bears like to go in the water.

Black bears like to go in trees.

What do brown bears AND black bears do?

All the bears make a home
here or here.

They sleep in the winter.

They have babies in the winter too.

Baby bears live with mom, they do not live with dad.

Baby bears will live with mom for over a year.

Can you see if this is a brown bear...

...or a black bear?

Bears Live Here

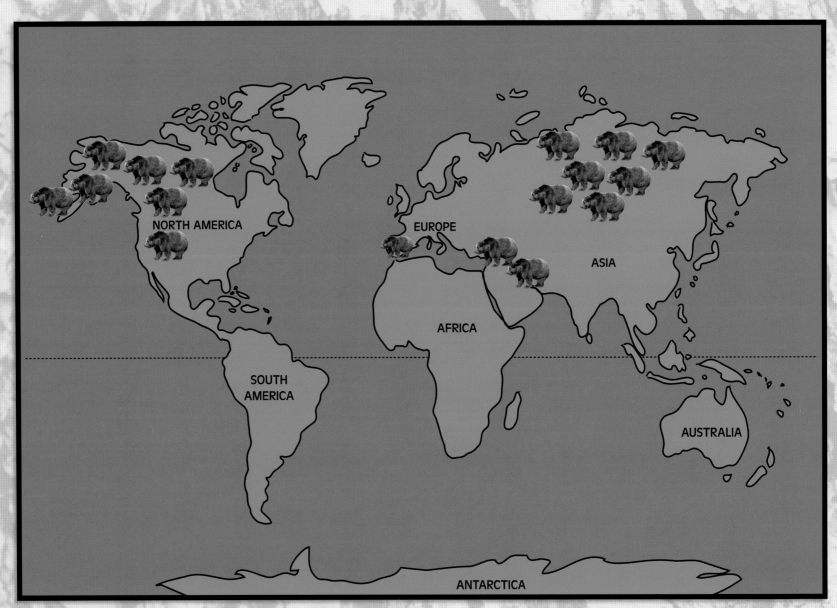

Bear Body Parts

ears

eyes

nose

mouth

legs

paws

claws

The Bear's Food Web

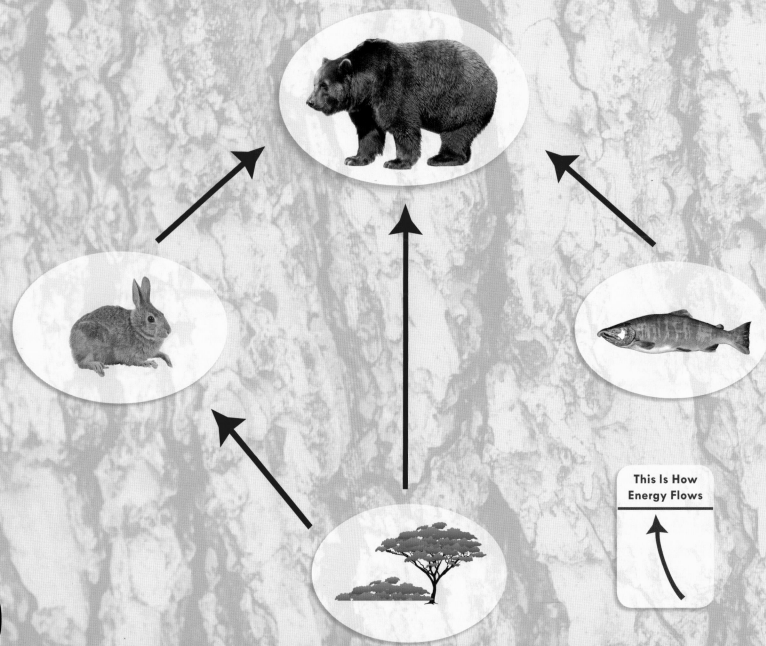

This Is How
Energy Flows

The Bear's Life Cycle

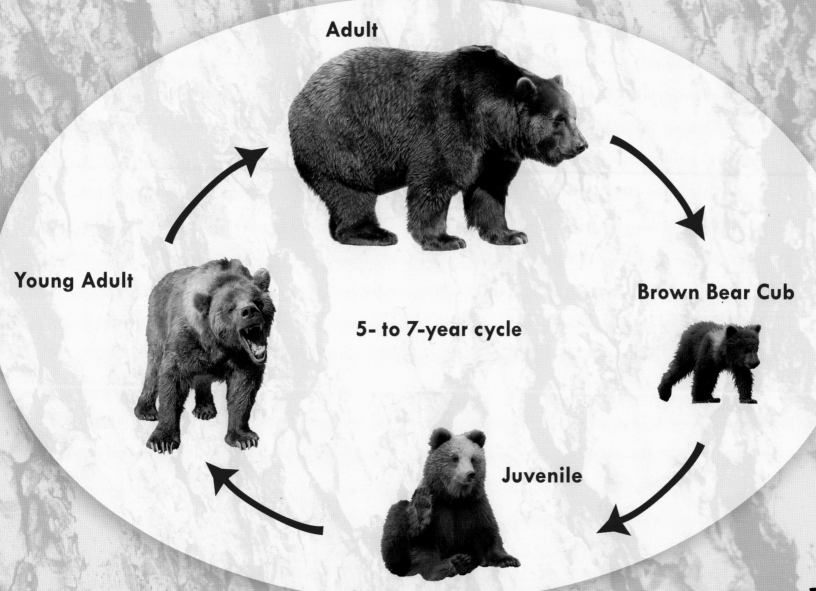

Adult

Young Adult

Brown Bear Cub

5- to 7-year cycle

Juvenile

Power Words
How many can you read?

a	big	do	here	it	make	see	too
all	black	eat	home	like	mom	some	what
and	brown	for	how	little	not	the	will
are	but	go	if	live	of	they	with
as	can	has	in	look	or	this	you
baby	dad	have	is	lots	over	to	

Bear Words

babies	ear	fish	sleep	summer	water	year
bear	fall	paws	spring	trees	winter	